Copyright ©2020 ARNOLD KUNTZ PH.L

CONTENTS

INTRODUCTION

What exactly does an anti-inflammatory diet consist of and how does it work?

What causes inflammation?

Healthy Dog Diets: Foods that Reduce Inflammation

Dog Food Ingredients that are Anti-inflammatory

Food that combat inflammation

Feeding an Arthritic Dog: Inflammatory and Anti-Inflammatory Foods

Dog arthritis

Nightshade Vegetables

Grains

Avoid Fillers

Foods that are anti-inflammatory

Homemade Recipe

How is the gut microbiome involved in inflammation?

How can diet lead to inflammation in your dog?

Food sensitivities

How can you lower your dog's risk for chronic inflammation?

The Difference between Acute and Chronic Inflammation

What Causes Chronic Inflammation?

What is a Functional Food?

What does energetically balanced mean for your dog?

Protein Choices

5 Disease-Fighting Foods for Your Dog

Foods to avoid if your dog has arthritis

Natural Foods & Supplements that Help Canine Arthritis

Foods to Avoid If Your Dog Has Arthritis

Treats and Table Scraps

Canned Food vs. Kibble

    Canned Dog Food – The Pros

    Canned Dog Food – The Cons

    Kibble Dog Food – The Pros

    The Cons of Kibble

Ingredients to Look for in Dog Food to Promote Healthy Joints

Supplements

    Foods and Supplements That May Help Dogs with Arthritis Pain

CONCLUSION

INTRODUCTION

Sometimes, the toughest part of watching your dog get older is seeing them slow down. They don't move with the same excitement and they're not as spry as the days they were a playful puppy.

This is often a direct result of joint pain and diminishing mobility as they age, which is an even greater challenge to treat because most dogs won't moan or whine as a result, letting you know they're in so much pain from those aging joints. The most common treatments are often pain medications and prescription drugs that can bring unwanted side effects like something as simple as a loss of appetite or even greater loss of energy for your dog. This is exactly why it's so important for pet owners to provide their pets with additional support in the form of natural remedies like CBD treatment and of course, a diet packed with anti-inflammatory foods.

WHAT EXACTLY DOES AN ANTI-INFLAMMATORY DIET CONSIST OF AND HOW DOES IT WORK?

First, it's important to understand inflammation and its connection to the painful degenerative joint disease, arthritis. Inflammation is a process in which the body's white blood cells protect it from infection by bacteria and viruses, attempting to heal wounds and injuries of all sorts. In this sense, inflammation is a valuable and necessary immune response. But sometimes, with diseases like arthritis, an inflammatory response when there is no outside bacteria to fight can cause damage to tissues and even digestive problems. Your immune system also releases chemical messengers called cytokines, the messengers within the body that regulate inflammation. According to Dr. Robert Zembroski, MD, a specialist in functional medicine, those cytokines can wreak havoc on neurotransmitters and affect the amygdala, which is a part of the brain that plays a heavy role in regulating and processing emotions. This can lead to triggering anxiety, depression, and even hallucinations. Research is backing these findings up by revealing higher levels of inflammation in people suffering from things like depression, suicidal thoughts, and PTSD in people. Further, Rheumatoid arthritis,

Psoriatic arthritis, and Gouty arthritis are just a few examples of the autoimmune diseases associated with these painful inflammation responses. Redness, swollen joints, joint pain, stiff joints, and even complete loss of joint function and mobility can result, turning the natural inflammation process into something that is dreadful to watch your beloved dog endure.

Food, as you may have guessed by now, can have a strong influence on inflammation. Inflammation of the chronic variety is internal inflammation that persists over time and serves no purpose for actually healing anything. It simply wreaks havoc on their joints as arthritis slowly wears tissue down over time, just as harmful to canines as it can be to humans. There are spices that contain certain nutrients that keep inflammation at bay, and those can, of course, be added to dishes within your dog's regular meals.

Some of these spices include:
-Cloves

-Ginger

-Rosemary

-Turmeric

-Paprika

As for the foods that can help with inflammation alone, you can often find the anti-inflammatory vitamins needed in many common dog foods. You don't necessarily have to go out of your way to create an entirely new daily menu for your dog just to make sure they're getting a balanced anti-inflammatory diet at the very least you can simply pay closer attention to the labels on the food you're already giving them. Look for foods with animal-based omega 3 fatty acids, which are often found the easiest in recipes that contain fish. In fact, many pet owners even go so far as to give their pets fish oil supplements in pill or capsule form. Research supports these fatty acids can also help your pet with skin conditions, allergies, kidney function, lymphoma, heart disease, and even cognitive function.

Berries, especially blueberries, and other fruits like papayas and cherries are helpful for relieving inflammation also. Aside from providing antioxidants, protecting cholesterol in your blood from being damaged, and maintaining healthy brain function, the specific antioxidant called anthocyanin fights inflammation. Anthocyanins stimulate the production of natural killer cells (NK cells), which help keep the immune system functioning at its best, which in turn regulates chronic inflammation. There are also other inflammatory markers that are reduced when certain berries and fruits are consumed, therefore lowering the risk of heart problems, making these an all-around good addition to your pup's diet.

For many of the same reasons, leafy greens and vegetables, including kale, spinach, broccoli, cauliflower, squash, pumpkin, bell peppers, and sweet potatoes can also help with inflammation as well. Similar to all those spices, many of these vegetables can also add a little bit of flavor to your dog's meal that they will enjoy. In fact, even adding more color to your dog's plate or bowl will tend to pique their appetite, making the entire dish more appealing to them simply with a splash of vibrant colors added by fruits and vegetables. As you of course know, many of their packaged dry and wet foods are very bland as far as the color spectrum is concerned, so just this little change of scenery for them will be an exciting treat.

As you can see, helping your dog get an anti-inflammatory diet doesn't require a ton of research, preparation, or really even changing their diet much overall. It's often simply a matter of adding in a few foods that offer extra vitamins and minerals with anti-inflammatory properties.

You can typically keep feeding your dog many of the same meals they'd get on a day-to-day basis and start mixing in new vegetables, fruits, or spices that you find they'll like. Over time, you'll start to notice which additions your dog prefers and which ones they don't love. And hopefully, in the process relieve some of the painful inflammation comes with arthritis.

WHAT CAUSES INFLAMMATION?

Inflammation can be caused by various different internal and external stressors. 'Stressors' are essentially anything which creates stress on or in the body.

Physical stressors

As an example, a physical stressor can be a nasty knock or fall. Excessive exercise can also cause inflammation. That creaky feeling after overdoing it at the gym two days ago? That's DOMS (Delayed Onset Muscle Soreness). Inflammation in your body is deployed to repair those torn muscle fibers. This is why it's important to give the occasional rest day to your dog.

External stressors

The best way to define an external stressor is by listing some:

Pollution from cars – Dogs walk around at exhaust pipe level

Chemicals that you apply to your dog's skin or coat, such as synthetic anti-flea or worm treatments

Humans get exposed to these issues with toiletries which can include toxic chemicals such as parabens. Read more about these from the hard working people at Breast

Internal stressors

These tend to be foods which cause inflammation in your dog. Examples of these include:

Food intolerances or allergies – Your dog's body sees certain foods it is intolerant to as an 'invader'. It launches an inflammatory response while it locks the food down to deal with it.

Inappropriate foods – Such as grains or lectins. More on why grains shouldn't be part of a balanced dog diet

Fats which have oxidized or are rancid. These fats oxidize when they exposed to the air. Rather than performing as those magical anti-inflammatory molecules, they become 'Pro-inflammatory'. That's why omega 3 fats is not included in our air-dried raw dry foods. In our Raw Frozen range, the omega 3's are already protected from heat, light and air. They are also minimally prepared, for maximum freshness.

HEALTHY DOG DIETS: FOODS THAT REDUCE INFLAMMATION

Chronic inflammation, which is internal inflammation that persists and serves no healing purpose, is linked to many health issues including obesity, heart disease, cancer, and arthritis. The inflammation that occurs after an injury is the body's natural response to the trauma. Its purpose it to flood the injury site with nourishment and kick start the healing process. Chronic inflammation serves no such purpose and is detrimental to overall health. There are many factors that can lead to chronic inflammation including lack of exercise, stress, and poor diet. Inflammation is harmful to the health of dogs just as it is to humans. One of the keys to keeping a dog's inflammation at bay is a healthy and varied diet. There are an assortment of spices and foods that can be a first line of defense against chronic inflammation. Some of the more commonly used foods in commercial pet food recipes are listed below.

DOG FOOD INGREDIENTS THAT ARE ANTI-INFLAMMATORY

Spices that combat inflammation Herbs and spices contain an assortment of vitamins and minerals, and can be a great way to prevent chronic inflammation. Some of the more powerful anti-inflammatory spices include:

Cloves

Ginger

Rosemary

Turmeric

Paprika

Besides being anti-inflammatory, these spices can improve the taste of the food. Furthermore, spices can act as natural preservatives, and can extend the freshness of dog food and eliminate the need for artificial (and potentially harmful) preservatives. If your dog's food does not contain these spices, consider sprinkling some in their dish when you are feeding.

FOOD THAT COMBAT INFLAMMATION

There are several foods that have anti-inflammatory properties, any of which are commonly found in dog food recipes.

Animal-based omega 3 fatty acids, like those found in fatty fish

Berries, especially blueberries, and many other fruits like papaya and cherries.

Leafy greens and vegetables, including kale, spinach, broccoli, cauliflower, squash, pumpkin, bell peppers, sweet potato.

These foods are great additions to any dog food recipe. Besides being anti-inflammatory, they provide a natural source of sweetness and flavor, which is much better than added sugars or other "natural flavors". Fruits and vegetables are also the preferred way to add color to dog food, and are a much better alternative than the artificial colors that are often found in the lower quality foods.

FEEDING AN ARTHRITIC DOG: INFLAMMATORY AND ANTI-INFLAMMATORY FOODS

DOG ARTHRITIS

When synovial fluid that separates the joints begins to thin, dogs will experience excruciating stiffness and pain associated with arthritis. In addition to a course of treatment, you can maximize your dog's quality of life by eliminating certain foods from his diet that can cause additional inflammation, while replacing them with healthier options.

NIGHTSHADE VEGETABLES

Vegetables of the nightshade family include eggplant, white potatoes, tomatoes, and peppers. These foods all contain glycoalkaloids, which are a type of chemical that can produce muscle spasms, aches, stiffness, and inflammation throughout the body if eaten regularly. For the normal person (or dog), symptoms are rarely noticed, however if already suffering from a joint condition then these foods can make matters much. Look for these ingredients listed in your pet's food (especially white potatoes), and switch to a different formulation if present.

GRAINS

Just as in humans, grains can cause inflammation in dogs, as well. Wheat, rye, and barley all contain gluten, which can aggravate arthritis symptoms. Gluten can be difficult to digest, leading the immune system to attack it as a "toxin." When the immune system reacts, inflammation is produced, and this leads to increased aches and pains. Look for grain free diets for your dog, especially those that list sweet potato as the main carbohydrate source.

AVOID FILLERS

Many dry dog foods available on the market contain fillers such as corn bran, grain by-products, soybean, peanut, cottonseed, or rice hulls, and modified corn starch. Not only are these foods nutritionally deplete, but they also negatively impact joint health by increasing the body's inflammatory response. Look for foods that contain whole ingredients, and always avoid words such as "bran" "hulls" "meal" or "by-product."

FOODS THAT ARE ANTI-INFLAMMATORY

You may be asking yourself what your dog can eat, after seeing the list of foods that he or she should avoid. Fortunately, there are many whole food options that can ease arthritis pain when fed regularly to your pet. These include celery, alfalfa, ginger, mango, papaya, blueberries, and kale, among others. Pet owners can blend these fruits and vegetables together to make a juice or smoothie and add them to the dog's daily diet.

HOMEMADE RECIPE

If the list of foods that dogs should not eat is too restrictive, consider making your dog's food at home. A common formulation for dogs with arthritis includes celery, carrots, zucchini, sweet potatoes, kale, spinach, quinoa, lentils, parsley, and apples. The exact amounts of each ingredient are not important, except that the overall product should contain 2 parts quinoa/lentils to 8 parts fruits/vegetables. Combine all ingredients together in a large pot and add enough water to cover all ingredients. Bring to a boil and let simmer on low for 1 hour or until quinoa and lentils are cooked. For additional protein, cooked chicken can be added, as well. This food can be used to replace traditional dry food, or used as a supplement.

HOW IS THE GUT MICROBIOME INVOLVED IN INFLAMMATION?

Genetics, metabolic diseases, parasites, food allergies, environmental stress, and bacterial overgrowth are all potential causes of chronic inflammation. But when the digestive system is affected, it makes sense to look closely at both diet and the gut microbiome. The gut microbiome is the collection of bacteria, yeasts, and other single-celled organisms that live in the digestive tract, helping to digest your dog's food and extract the nutrients.

In both animals and humans, the gut microbiome also plays a vital role in the development of a healthy immune system, and diet influences which types of bacteria inhabit the digestive tract. Some of these bacteria actually stimulate inflammation in order to fight harmful invader organisms. Other gut bacteria reduce inflammation. Faecalibacterium, for example, has been shown to have an anti-inflammatory function in humans. In dogs, deficiencies in Faecalibacterium have been associated with inflammatory bowel disease (IBD). In addition to a rich microbial community, a healthy digestive tract has a mucus barrier that only certain substances can pass through. But when the gut's defenses malfunction, this barrier becomes "leaky," allowing pathogens and antigens (molecules that stimulate the immune system) to be absorbed into the lining of the intestines. The antigens trigger an immune system response, and the resulting inflammation irritates the intestinal wall, making it even less able to keep toxins out and leading to further inflammation.

The gut's normal defenses can break down for many reasons but there is an especially clear connection between chronic inflammation and antibiotic medications, which can cause drastic imbalances in the microbiome by killing off beneficial bacteria along with harmful ones. If your dog needs to take antibiotics, consider tracking their gut health and taking steps to increase their gut bacteria diversity.

HOW CAN DIET LEAD TO INFLAMMATION IN YOUR DOG?

The canine and human gut microbiomes have been shown to have significant similarities, so a lot of what we know about the connection between diet and chronic inflammation in humans also applies to dogs. In humans, diets that are high in saturated fat, Trans fats, sugar, and/or refined carbohydrates have been shown to lead to an increase in inflammatory symptoms. High-calorie diets also directly stimulate inflammation because fat tissue is rich in immune cells. Many studies have demonstrated that more fat tissue results in more chronic inflammation. In both dogs and humans, the ratio of proteins and carbohydrates in the diet has a significant influence on the balance of gut microbes and therefore also on levels of fat tissue. In one study, dogs who were fed a high-protein, low-carbohydrate diet not only had better digestive health than dogs on a low-protein, high-carbohydrate diet, they also showed beneficial changes in the levels of bacteria that regulate fat absorption.

Though a high-fat diet promotes increases in both body weight and inflammation, the role of polyunsaturated fats, such as omega-3 and omega-6 fatty acids, is more complicated. Many studies have shown that a high ratio of omega-3 to omega-6 fatty acids can lead to a reduction in inflammation. As a result of these studies, pet owners are often advised to feed a diet that is higher in omega-3 and lower in omega-6.

FOOD SENSITIVITIES

Food allergies and intolerances are another connection between diet and inflammation. If your dog has the symptoms of inflammatory bowel disease (IBD), your veterinarian's first step will likely be to determine whether any food sensitivities are involved. Your dog may be reacting to a particular source of either protein or carbohydrates or to one or more of the many additives and preservatives found in most pet foods.

In both dogs and humans, food allergies or sensitivities can result from an imbalance in the gut microbiome. Low levels of Coprococcus and Oscillospira bacteria in the gut, for example, as observed in individuals with food allergies, whereas the presence of Clostridiales in the intestinal tract makes the host organism less vulnerable to developing food allergies.

HOW CAN YOU LOWER YOUR DOG'S RISK FOR CHRONIC INFLAMMATION?

Feed a diet that's relatively high in protein and low in carbohydrates.

Minimize your dog's consumption of highly processed foods that contain a lot of additives or preservatives.

Work with your vet to identify any food sensitivities that may be affecting your dog's health.

Maintain your dog's weight at a healthy level.

Supplement your dog's diet with more omega-3 and less omega-6 (for example, with fish oil).

Feed only dog-appropriate treats. If your dog has food sensitivities, try PupJoy, which offers treats for dogs on special diets.

THE DIFFERENCE BETWEEN ACUTE AND CHRONIC INFLAMMATION

As mentioned above there is a difference between acute and chronic inflammation. Inflammation is a totally normal function of the dog's body. Acute inflammation happens when there is an immediate need for the dog's body to heal itself. An example of this might be when your dog runs a fever or swelling of one of your dog's limbs after an injury. These are signs that the dog's body is recovering. And once the dog's body has done its anti-inflammatory job, the signs of inflammation (the fever, the swelling) disappear. Back to normal.

Chronic inflammation is different because it doesn't happen right away and is the type of inflammation that can lead to serious damage and diseases. It can take days, weeks, months, or even years to start noticing symptoms of chronic inflammation. An example of this is heart disease. Heart disease is actually a disease caused (or greatly exacerbated) by chronic inflammation. The thin layer of cells that line blood vessel walls, called the endothelium, can be damaged by anything harmful entering the bloodstream (i.e. pollution, pesticides, processed food). This repetitive injury to the endothelium causes the immune system to dispatch white blood cells, which multiply; this is how inflammation is supposed to function. But when these inflammatory cells stay within the blood vessel walls for too long over an extended period of time, they cause the build-up of dangerous plaques. And when these plaques explode inside of an artery, a heart attack or stroke may occur. Heart disease is just one possible product of chronic inflammation, but the idea is the same for so many diseases and health issues: when the dog's body thinks it is under attack by a stressor, the immune system fights back. Inflammation is a sign that the immune system is on the attack due to real or perceived stress.

Some Symptoms of Chronic Inflammation:
Digestive issues

Low energy

Body pain, especially in the joints

Skin issues and chronic ear infections

Autoimmune disease, like arthritis, thyroid, celiac disease

High blood glucose

High cholesterol

Allergies to food ingredients and environmental exposure

WHAT CAUSES CHRONIC INFLAMMATION?

The good news is that chronic inflammation is largely due to a poor diet. (that's good news, because it can be fixed nutritionally!). The most common causes of chronic inflammation are digestive issues, a highly processed diet, toxins, allergens, infections, and chronic stress.

Another common cause of chronic inflammation is a damaged gut lining, often called "leaky gut syndrome." Without a healthy mucosal lining, the tight cellular junctions of the gut weaken, allowing food particles and bacteria to pass out of the small intestine and into the bloodstream.

These food particles are not supposed to be in the bloodstream and so they appear foreign to the body, often triggering an immune response. "Leaky gut syndrome" can be caused by chronic stress, food sensitivities, and gut infections. So, the health of the gut is really important here.

WHAT IS A FUNCTIONAL FOOD?

Functional foods are foods that have a potentially positive effect on health beyond basic nutrition. The research focus has shifted more to the identification of biologically active components in foods that have the potential to optimize physical and mental well-being and which may also reduce the risk of disease. A familiar example of a functional food found is parsley because of its anti-inflammatory properties that help promote good kidney health and antimicrobial properties that promote good urinary health.

Functional foods include:
Conventional foods such as grains, fruits, vegetables, and nuts.

Modified foods such as yogurt.

Medical foods such as special formulations of foods for certain health conditions.

Foods for special dietary use such as anti-inflammatory or hypo-allergenic foods.

Chronic inflammation, which is an internal inflammation that persists and serves no healing purpose, is linked to many health issues including obesity, heart disease, cancer, and arthritis. Chronic inflammation serves no such purpose and is detrimental to overall health. Chronic inflammation in dogs is as harmful to their health just as it is to humans. Lack of exercise, stress, and poor diet are the causes. One of the keys to keeping a dog's inflammation at bay is a fresh, natural and varied species appropriate diet.

Ginger is used to combat inflammation and settles the stomach. Herbs contain an assortment of vitamins and minerals and can be a great way to prevent chronic inflammation. Besides being anti-inflammatory herbs can improve the taste of the food. Furthermore, herbs can act as natural preservatives and can extend the freshness of dog food and eliminate the need for artificial (and potentially harmful) preservatives. Ginger is recognized as the best anti-nausea herb and is well tolerated by dogs. It acts as a digestive tonic, relieving stomach aches and intestinal gas. It also stimulates the digestive juices and helps expel worms.

There are several other foods that have anti-inflammatory properties:

● Animal-based omega 3 fatty acids, like those found in fatty fish

● Leafy greens and vegetables, including broccoli, squash, beets, zucchini and pumpkin.

WHAT DOES ENERGETICALLY BALANCED MEAN FOR YOUR DOG?

The old adage that "you are what you eat" applies here. Food is classified as having various properties such as cooling, warming, etc. The cooling foods help to bring down the inflammation throughout the body. Foods like venison and lamb are considered the warmest of proteins and, to an allergic dog, would greatly increase the heat in the body and the allergic reaction. Incorporating cooling foods into an allergic dog's diet will help to resolve the underlying disharmony that is causing the reaction.

PROTEIN CHOICES

80/20 Beef is recommended because of its neutral properties and most dogs are not sensitive to a good quality grass fed beef. You should consider using Cooling proteins if beef cannot be tolerated. For variety, you also can use fish as an alternative. Small fatty fish such as whitefish, Herring, sardines, smelt or wild caught fish like mackerel. Pork Liver is included in this diet instead of chicken liver because of its neutrality.

5 DISEASE-FIGHTING FOODS FOR YOUR DOG

Fish Oil

Foods rich in omega-3 polyunsaturated fatty acids have been studied extensively for their role in controlling inflammation in a variety of species. These fatty acids have been shown to help in the management of kidney disease, joint disease, skin inflammation, and more. Many pet foods contain omega-3 fatty acids, he says, but not all of them. In addition, the amount added to [over-the-counter] products may not be sufficient to provide the desired beneficial effects.

The type of omega-3 fatty acids you feed your dog is also important. Omega-3 fatty acids from plant sources such as flax (a source of alpha-Linolenic acid) are inefficiently metabolized to eicosapentaenoic acid (EPA) and docosahexaenoic acid (DHA) in dogs and cats."EPA and DHA are the beneficial omega-3 fatty acids in terms of impact on the inflammatory process. This is why most veterinarians recommend omega-3 supplements derived from certain types of fish oil. Specially-formulated diets with appropriate amounts of EPA and DHA are also available by checking with your vet. Supplements are an option, but there are some things you should be aware of before buying a bottle. The manufacturer should have adequate quality control practices in place to ensure their products are free from toxins and metal contamination. Contacting the manufacturer to receive information on quality control and product testing is recommended when choosing a new omega-3 or fish oil supplement.

There are dozens of omega-3 supplements on the market, many of which formulated for humans. But there are solid reasons why you should opt for supplements made for pets instead. Many human products are supplemented with high levels of vitamin A or D, and over-supplementation may be risky. Fish oil is a source of extra fat calories, and in very high doses may have adverse effects on your dog. For these reasons, consult with a vet or board-certified veterinary nutritionist first.

If you're not a fan of supplements or your dog food doesn't contain omega-3s, consider steaming, grilling, or baking a piece of fish for your canine companion. Be mindful of the type of fish you choose, as some varieties are higher in mercury than others. Salmon is a good option since it is typically high in omega-3s but low in mercury.

Vegetables
Leafy green and yellow-orange vegetables, such as carrots, may decrease the risk of bladder cancer in certain dogs, a 2005 study of Scottish Terriers suggested. The goal of the study was to determine how vegetables (and supplements) might impact the development of transitional cell carcinoma (TCC) in Scottish Terriers. The scientists compared their findings of 92 Scottie dogs with confirmed cases of TCC, to those of 83 Scottie dogs with other conditions like parasitic infections and skin disease. Dogs who were fed veggies at least three times per week (carrots were the most often used) saw a reduction in the risk of developing TCC.

The scientists suspect bioflavanoids, dietary fiber, plant sterols, and other anti-carcinogenic substances (known as phyto-nutrients) present in these vegetables may inhibit or slow down the progression of cancer.

Yellow-orange vegetables used in the study (aside from carrots) included pumpkin, squash, and sweet potato. Leafy green vegetables included lettuce, salad greens, spinach, collard greens, and parsley. Raditic also recommends giving dogs swiss chard, turnip greens, beet greens, kale, and dandelion greens.

Mushrooms

Mushrooms contain polysaccharopeptides (PSP), which researchers believe have tumor-fighting properties. There is some evidence that they can improve immune responses.

There's a lot of data on how eating mushrooms can impact humans, and researchers at the University Of Pennsylvania School Of Veterinary Medicine in Philadelphia ran a trial on dogs with hemangiosarcoma, an aggressive cancer affecting the spleen.

The study involved researchers asking pet parents to feed their dogs capsules containing extracts from the Yunzhi mushroom every day. Each month, they brought their dogs to the university's Ryan Veterinary Hospital for follow up visits. It was founded out that the compound was effective at fighting the tumors, without needing any accompanying treatments.

If you do want to offer your canine companion mushrooms, it's important to keep in mind that some types of mushrooms are poisonous for dogs. Always talk to your veterinarian before adding mushrooms to your dog's diet.

Fiber

In some cases, veterinarians may recommend feeding oatmeal or lentils as part of a high-fiber diet. Flax, psyllium, or chia seeds can also be used to supplement your dog's diet. Fiber can help your dog feel full, and ultimately aid with weight loss. Keeping your dog lean is important. Obesity can shorten your dog's lifespan, and is linked with an assortment of diseases, including joint, liver, and respiratory disease. Fiber is also essential for maintaining gastrointestinal health, as it helps support the gut microflora. A healthy gut is linked with strengthened immunity, a factor in warding off disease.

Pet foods are often supplemented with fiber sources, such as beet pulp, psyllium, guar gum, and grain hulls. You can also try adding a small spoonful of plain oatmeal to your dog's regular food. There are some precautions to take when choosing foods and products with fiber. They may have negative effects in some patients, as excess fiber may reduce nutrient bioavailability, and may even cause discomfort or flatulence. There is also warning against feeding products that contain additives like xylitol (a sugar substitute), which is toxic to dogs.

Fruits

Veterinary nutritionists will often recommend that their clients feed fruits to their dogs as part of a sound nutritional plan. These recommendations are made because these fresh fruits and vegetables may provide trace nutrients or compounds that we have yet to discover, or that are not abundant in commercial pet food. Giving fruits and vegetables over commercial pet treats. If an owner is giving blueberries (or carrots, etc.), to their dog, we then know exactly what it is and where it came from." It can be difficult to identify the sources of all the ingredients some of which have questionable nutritional value in commercial pet treats.

The phyto-nutrients contained in blueberries and other fruits may help prevent cancer. This is one reason it is recommended that people train their puppies to have a taste for vegetables in particular, and also fruits. (No onions, garlic, grapes, or raisins, of course, which are toxic for dogs.) Fruits are also suggested because they are low-calorie treats and there is a canine obesity problem.

A general serving size for dogs, consists of five blueberries. Other fruits recommended include a whole medium-sized strawberry, or an inch of banana (this is an approximate serving for a 20-pound dog).

There is no one food currently known to guarantee that your dog will remain disease-free. Until research catches up, vets stress the importance of a balanced diet. Ensuring your dog has adequate amounts of nutrients provided by foods like fish, carrots, mushrooms, oatmeal, and blueberries can go a long way to ensuring she remains your healthy companion for a long time.

FOODS TO AVOID IF YOUR DOG HAS ARTHRITIS

Joint and mobility issues, like arthritis, are some of the most common health problems among dogs. Arthritis symptoms in your pup can range from being hardly noticeable to completely debilitating, and it can be difficult to watch your best friend's mobility decline. While unfortunately canine arthritis can't be completely "cured" (once the cartilage in your dog's joint/s has been damaged, it is rare that it's able to fully repair itself again), there are many things you can do as a pet parent to help keep their symptoms on the lower end of the spectrum and feeding them an anti-inflammatory diet is one of the most important. Depending on what you choose to feed or not feed your dog, their food can either act as a medicine or a toxin. It can help alleviate the symptoms of disease, or fuel them. With just a little awareness and effort on your part, you can begin feeding your dog a diet that helps fight the progression of arthritis, alleviates their discomfort, and contributes to their well-being on every level.

Your No 1 Goal: Reducing Inflammation
All forms of canine arthritis cause chronic inflammation in the joints, which leads to pain in the affected areas. Basically, inflammation of the joints in dogs is simply another way of saying your dog is suffering from arthritis and it's causing them pain. The more inflammation in your dog's joints, the more pain they experience. Inflammation of the joints in dogs occurs when the

cartilage within a joint is damaged, either from an acute injury or from wear and tear over the years. A normal joint will have a thin layer of cartilage covering the bones, and will be lubricated with joint fluid ensuring the joint glides smoothly and freely without any friction or discomfort. A joint with arthritis becomes rough and the bone surfaces of the joint rub together, causing inflammation. The joint becomes stiffer and limited in its mobility, which mirrors itself in the stiff gait and limited mobility that pet parents of arthritic dogs are only too familiar with. When your pup ingests something that causes an inflammatory response in their joints, this causes the tissues to swell even more, which then puts painful pressure on the nerves. Feeding an anti-inflammatory diet is one of the easiest and most natural ways to combat this chronic inflammation so your pet starts to feel relief. So which foods should you favor to fight inflammation, and which should you avoid to prevent contributing to it?

NATURAL FOODS & SUPPLEMENTS THAT HELP CANINE ARTHRITIS

It is important to know that nature provides an arsenal of whole foods that are inflammation-fighting powerhouses that can help alleviate the symptoms of canine arthritis. While we often think of these things veggies, fruits, etc. As "people food," they are both safe and extremely beneficial in managing your dog's arthritis pain.

Here's a few number of dog supplements for arthritic dogs:
Whole Foods

Fiber-filled veggies: Sweet potato, acorn squash, pumpkin

Antioxidant-packed fruits: Blueberries, cherries, peeled apple, cantaloupe

Vitamin-rich veggies: Broccoli, cauliflower, zucchini

Leafy greens: Spinach, kale, collards

Fatty fish: Salmon, mackerel, tuna, sardines

Lean protein: Chicken, turkey

Oils

Omega-3 oils: Fish oil, green lipped mussel oil

Coconut oil (mix in with dog's food or use to sauté dog's veggies)

Flaxseed oil (drizzle over dog's food)

Herbs and Spices

Fresh ginger root

Turmeric (fresh root or powdered)

Cinnamon

Parsley (bonus = breath freshener!)

FOODS TO AVOID IF YOUR DOG HAS ARTHRITIS

While whole foods from nature are wonderful at helping alleviate your dog's arthritis pain, we understand that most pet parents don't always have time to feed veggies, fruits, and freshly prepared proteins at every meal and sometimes you need the convenience of canned food or kibble. The trick lies in knowing how to choose the right canned food or kibble for an arthritic dog. While many processed dog foods contain refined ingredients, added sugars, and harmful preservatives that all contribute to painful inflammation in your dog's joints, knowing what ingredients to avoid will help you read and understand the labels to make the best choice for your pet.

Here are 5 foods to avoid if your dog has arthritis:

1. Grains

If your dog has arthritis, grain-free food may be the way to go. Many processed commercial dog foods contain grains such as wheat, rice, soy, and spelt, which can cause your dog's blood sugar levels to fluctuate and increase painful swelling. Limiting the grains in your dog's diet can decrease their inflammation. However, please talk to your veterinarian before making any switches to your dog's diet. There has been controversy surrounding grain-free diets so please consult your vet.

2. Corn

Corn is a somewhat controversial dog food topic, and staple ingredient and filler in many dog foods. Corn has a high carbohydrate content and while it provides a quick source of energy, it can also cause a sensitivity that leads to inflammation for some dogs. You would not see an immediate adverse reaction upon your dog ingesting it, but it could gradually worsen your dog's inflammation over time.

3. Omega-6 Fatty Acids

Most dogs who eat a commercial diet will have a plethora of omega 6-fatty acids in their system. This is because omega-6s, which are high in cheaper oils such as corn, soybean, safflower, sunflower, and canola oils, are less costly and more readily available for pet food manufacturers. Also found in meat and poultry, omega-6s are part of a normal dog's diets, but should be kept to a minimum for dogs who suffer from arthritis. The body converts excess omega-6s such as linoleic acid in the body to arachidonic acid, which is highly inflammatory to arthritis sufferers. An easy and effective way to remedy this imbalance is to provide a high-quality daily omega-3 supplement. Omega-3 fatty acids produce hormones that decrease harmful low-grade chronic inflammation and work alongside omega-6 in such a way to maintain optimal health.

4. Fatty Proteins

This one is on the list because it is extremely detrimental for an arthritic dog to be overweight (and there's a good chance they are, as obesity affects more than 50% of dogs in the U.S.).

While protein is important in an arthritic dog's diet because it supports strong muscles to protect joints, if they are carrying even a little bit of extra weight, try to favor lean proteins such as chicken, turkey, or grass-fed meat. While fatty fish such as salmon and tuna contain beneficial omega-3s, your main goal should be to provide a healthy diet while keeping calories down. It's extremely important to understand as a pet parent to an arthritic dog just how crucial it is to keep them at an ideal weight. Decreasing the load on your dog's joints is critical, and even the slightest bit of excess weight will compound their arthritis pain, decreasing their quality of life.

5. Added Salts, Sugars, and Artificial Additives

As a general rule, the more processed a food is, the more likely it is to contribute to inflammation. By definition, all manufactured dog foods are going to be processed to an extent, so it's important to choose one that contains no added salts, sugars, or artificial additives, which are basically an unnecessary recipe for increased inflammation. When choosing a food for your arthritic dog, be sure to read the label carefully and avoid these 5 foods as much as possible to ensure what they're eating act as medicine in their body, not a toxin.

TREATS AND TABLE SCRAPS

If you're like most pet parents, the occasional treats and table scraps are one way you show your dog how much you love them. Giving a well-deserved treat is such a wonderful way for you to bond with your pup that we actually never recommend you stop giving your dog treats, even if they're overweight.

However, it is recommended you make a few modifications to how you give treats, especially for arthritic dogs. Remember that the more processed something is, the more likely it is to lead to painful inflammation. Dog treats are notorious for being highly-processed, containing high amounts of salt, fat, and sugar. There are several natural alternatives that your dog will enjoy just as much think crunchy baby carrots, sweet pieces of cut up fruit, or delightfully chewy dehydrated veggies. If you absolutely have to give your pup a treat out of a bag, find one with the most natural ingredients possible and break it in half or even smaller pieces to keep the calorie count down.

The same goes for table scraps the more natural, the better. Before you give your pup anything from your plate, ask how far it is from its original form. For example, pasta, white bread, and cheese aren't found anywhere in nature, but eggs, blueberries, and cauliflower are. Find healthy alternatives that your dog still enjoys and stick to those. Your dog may get momentary pleasure from chomping down a chunk of cheese, but it's not worth contributing to painful inflammation.

CANNED FOOD VS. KIBBLE

You're now armed with the info you need to make an informed choice about the ingredients in your dog's food. The next question may then be, canned food or kibble? In short, the canned food vs. kibble debate is not one that has a cut-and-dried answer. Canned and kibble dog food both have their good and bad points. Which food you decide to feed is really a personal decision based on many factors including what your vet advises.

CANNED DOG FOOD – THE PROS

Canned dog foods typically have much less grain and carbs in them than kibble foods (a huge plus for arthritic dogs), even if you aren't buying grain-free canned food. This is because kibbles require a large amount of carbs as much as 50% so they can go through the machinery and be extruded into kibble form. Since this process isn't necessary for canned food, these typically have more meat protein which are good for your dog depending on their sources – remember, try to stick to lean proteins for arthritic dogs.

Canned dog food also typically has fewer chemical additives than kibble, as well as less artificial flavoring and coloring which can all contribute to harmful inflammation. Canned foods don't need the kind of preservatives that kibble does because they are preserved through the canning process. Also, canned food contains more water than kibble, often being around 75% liquid, which helps your dog stay hydrated. Proper hydration is key for keeping joints adequately lubricated, allowing them to move and flex as needed. Dehydration can lead to stiff tendons and ligaments, which can cause heightened pain in arthritic dogs and increase the risk of injury.

CANNED DOG FOOD – THE CONS

One of the main cons of canned dog food is that it often uses thickening agents to make the food hold its shape. One of these thickeners is carrageenan, which has been associated with inflammatory bowel disease (IBD), acid reflux, and intestinal ulceration. Also, most dog food cans are lined with Bisphenol-A (BPA), which has been associated with some health problems in people. And there's the cost as well. Canned food is almost always more expensive than kibble of the same quality, and cost can add up quickly especially if you have a large dog or multiple dogs.

KIBBLE DOG FOOD – THE PROS

The main advantages of kibble are cost and convenience. Kibble usually costs less per ounce than canned dog food, even when you compare foods of the same quality. Kibble is also more convenient to feed (you don't need to open cans) and easier to store.

THE CONS OF KIBBLE

Most dog owners in the U.S. choose to feed kibble dog food because of lower cost and higher convenience. If you choose to do so for your arthritic dog, be sure you're feeding one with quality ingredients and look for a product with higher protein, lower carbs, which typically means better nutrition.

INGREDIENTS TO LOOK FOR IN DOG FOOD TO PROMOTE HEALTHY JOINTS

We've covered which ingredients to avoid in your arthritic dog's food – whether it be kibble or canned food so which ingredients should you favor? Here are some of the top nutrients that decrease inflammation and contribute to healthy joints

1. Omega 3-Fatty Acids
As mentioned, omega-3 fatty acids are a powerful, natural way to reduce inflammation and balance the omega-6s in your dog's body. While many dog foods and supplement use fish oil as an omega-3 ingredient, by far our favorite source is the green lipped mussel, found in our Flexerna supplement, which contains a more diverse omega-3 profile to efficiently and effectively combat joint pain and inflammation.

2. Lean Protein
As mentioned, lean protein plays an important role in taking care of the muscles and soft tissues that support the joints and contribute to the overall health of your dog's musculoskeletal system, without as much of a risk of packing on harmful pounds. Look for chicken, turkey, or grass-fed meat.

3. Glucosamine

Glucosamine is the oldest and most researched ingredient in the joint supplement world, and is often added to dog foods aimed at keeping joints healthy. An amino sugar that is essential for maintaining healthy cartilage and joint function, glucosamine is naturally produced by your dog's body. But over time, their natural production becomes inadequate at preventing joint damage and must be supplemented. If you have an older dog or a pup suffering from arthritis, be sure to help boost their reserve of this crucial nutrient.

4. Chondroitin

Chondroitin is a cartilage component that promotes water retention (remember, hydration is key!) and elasticity needed for mobility and inhibits many of the degradative enzymes that break down cartilage and joint fluid.

5. Methylsulfonylmethane

Methylsulfonylmethane (or MSM) is a naturally-occurring, easily-absorbed sulfur that is an essential building block for all cell membranes. In a nutshell, it is a cell rejuvenator, antioxidant, and joint healer that is highly effective at relieving pain and inflammation.

6. Hyaluronic Acid

Hyaluronic acid (or HA) is a gel-like substance that is naturally produced by your dog's body, serving as a shock absorber and helping to lubricate their joint fluid. In older dogs, highly active dogs, or dogs that have suffered an injury, HA can become damaged and lead to joint issues. Supplementing HA has been shown to be effective in replacing damaged HA in the joints that commonly occurs from overuse, age, or trauma.

7. Cetyl Myristoleate

A relative of the omega-9 fatty acid found in olive oil, cetyl myristoleate is a completely natural long chain esterified fatty acids found in certain animals, such as cows, whales, beavers, and mice – but not dogs (or humans, for that matter). It is a wonderful anti-inflammatory, as well as a pain reliever and immune system modulator.

8. Vitamin C (Ascorbic Acid)

Unlike humans, dogs' bodies are able to create their own vitamin C, but dogs with joint problems need more than what their bodies produce naturally. This antioxidant protects against free radicals that accelerate the aging process and aids in the absorption of the other ingredients.

While these are found in many quality canned and kibble dog foods geared towards joint health, you can also provide them to your dog in supplement form. If you want a shortcut to providing your pup with the last 6 ingredients on the list above, GlycanAid contains them all in one convenient joint supplement.

Simply put, food can do one of two things for an arthritic dog: it can soothe their system and promote healing, or it can be toxic, fueling imbalance and disease. The choice is up to you. Armed with this information, you can now begin feeding your arthritic dog an anti-inflammatory diet that will assist in preventing further deterioration of their joints and managing arthritis pain to help them live full, happy lives.

SUPPLEMENTS

Essentially, quality joint supplements contain ingredients that stimulate the growth of cartilage, lubricate joints, inhibit cartilage-destroying enzymes, and more to improve the health of the joint. While omega supplements, on the other hand, focus mainly on reducing chronic inflammation, which reduces a healthy dog's risk for joint problems and other countless diseases, helps relieve arthritis pain, and promotes healthy heart, brain, and immune function.

FOODS AND SUPPLEMENTS THAT MAY HELP DOGS WITH ARTHRITIS PAIN

Diet becomes especially important for dogs with arthritis because excess body fat strains joints and bones, causing even more discomfort. Moderate exercise, massage, acupuncture, and medication are all tools in addition to certain foods that can help with arthritis pain. Consult your veterinarian about all of these options before you make any dietary or lifestyle changes and form a plan that works for you and your dog. Here are ten natural foods and supplements that may work as remedies for arthritis pain in dogs.

1. Sweet Potatoes

Sweet potatoes are high in beta-carotene, which is helpful in fighting inflammation. They also contain amino acids, which aid in building muscle that may have started to fade with old age and lack of exercise due to the arthritis pain. Amino acids increase antioxidant activity in the body, which fights cell damage that contributes to a number of conditions.

2. Fish Oil

Fish oil is rich in omega-3 fatty acids that act as an anti-inflammatory and increase joint mobility. It can also add calories to your dog's diet, so make sure you balance it with other calorie sources to avoid harmful weight gain. Fish oil has a host of other benefits for your dog's body, which is a bonus. Many owners use it to keep their dog's skin and coat healthy. However, make sure to avoid cod liver oil as it is too high in vitamins A and D.

3. Turmeric

Turmeric contains circumin and other anti-inflammatory compounds that reduce pain and stiffness.

Circumin can also slow cell damage from free radicals with its antioxidant properties, as well as inhibiting enzymes that are known to cause swelling and pain.

4. Glucosamine and Chondroitin Sulfate

Glucosamine is a compound of sugar and an amino acid, and it's naturally produced by the body. It's extracted from shellfish, and it aids in the production of joint lubricants and shock absorption for healthy cartilage and joints. Glucosamine is often paired with chondroitin sulfate, which is naturally found in cartilage. These supplements help the body repair cartilage and protect it from breaking down.

5. Ginger

Ginger is in the same family as turmeric and has many of the same benefits. It acts as an anti-inflammatory that can reduce pain. Ginger contains gingerol, which has been shown in lab tests to relieve the pain associated with arthritis by preventing inflammation and joint destruction.

6. Alfalfa

Alfalfa contains antioxidants that prevent cellular damage, which can contribute to joint degradation. It also has anti-inflammatory properties that reduce swelling and pain. It's rich in protein, nutrients, and vitamins, and has a lot of other health benefits for your dog as an added bonus.

7. Papaya

Like many fruits, papaya has antioxidant properties that prevent cell damage, and they're high in vitamin C. They have the added benefit of being lower in citric acid that other fruits that have antioxidants, making them easier on the stomach and more digestible for dogs. Mangoes have similar properties to papayas and can also help fight the pain of arthritis.

8. Blueberries

Blueberries are the strongest antioxidant fruit grown in North America and are great for fighting inflammation and other conditions like cancer. They are also a good source of vitamin C. Additionally, the silicon in blueberries helps strengthen bones and the connective tissue in joints.

9. Celery

Celery is an anti-inflammatory that's low in calories, which helps with keeping weight in balance and preventing additional strain on joints. It's also high in antioxidants and fiber, which is important in fighting obesity and osteoporosis that can worsen the pain of arthritis. The amino acids, calcium, and vitamins it contains help keep bones and joints strong. Celery also helps move uric acid out of the body. Uric acid can worsen arthritis.

10. Coconut Oil

Coconut is an anti-inflammatory that helps to lubricate joints. It contains valuable fatty acids and fights viral, bacterial, and fungal infections that contribute to arthritis pain. Coconut oil can also give your dog an energy boost that can help with moderate exercise to keep up muscle and fight obesity.

CONCLUSION

Inflammation is one way a healthy immune system helps the body heal injuries and fight off foreign invaders, such as bacteria and viruses. When cell damage or a pathogen is detected, the immune system increases blood flow to the area, sending white blood cells and extra fluid to the surrounding tissues. The resulting Inflammation with its physical symptoms of redness, swelling, and heat stimulates tissue repair and protects against infection. But when the immune system reacts abnormally, treating the body's own cells or an element of the diet as a foreign invader, inflammation can become chronic. Chronic inflammation in your dog's digestive system can disrupt the gut's normal functions, causing vomiting, diarrhea, reduced appetite, weight loss, and nutrient deficiencies.